Blackroots Science

Level 2

Personal Journal

Copyright © 2018
Blackroots Science Publications

All rights reserved. This book or any portion thereof may not be reproduced in any manner whatsoever without the express written permission of the publisher except for the use of brief quotations in a book review or scholarly journal.

First Printing: 2018

ISBN-13: 978-1719405744

ISBN-10:   1719405743

Blackroots Science Publications
California, United States of America

Printed in the United States

www.blackrootscience.com

publisher@blackrootscience.com

	1st Stage - Planting	2nd Stage - Nurturing	3rd Stage - Harvesting
Lesson 1 **Observations**	Done between 6pm - midnight Every 3 days Do Exercises 1-7 Recall Exercises 7-1 Take 7-10 day break Read 12 DP Statements	Done between 12noon - 6pm Every 2 days Do Exercises 8-14 Recall Exercises 14-8 Take 7-10 day break Read 12 DP Statements	Done between 6am - 12noon Every day Do Exercises 15-21 Recall Exercises 21-15 Take 7-10 day break Read 12 DP Statements

3-Day Review During Break
Day1: Review Exercises 21-15 for 1 hour, 3-7 min per exercise
Day2: Review Exercises 14-8 for 1 hour, 3-7 min per exercise
Day3: Review Exercises 7-1 for 1 hour, 3-7 min per exercise

	1st Stage (Planting)	2nd Stage (Nurturing)	3rd Stage (Harvesting)
Lesson 2 **Observations**	Done between 12noon - 6pm Every 2 days Do Exercises 22-28 Recall Exercises 28-22 Take 7-10 day break Read 24 DP Statements	Done between 6pm - midnight Every 3 days Do Exercises 29-35 Recall Exercises 35-29 Take 7-10 day break Read 24 DP Statements	Done between 12noon - 6pm Every 2 days Do Exercises 36-42 Recall Exercises 42-36 Take 7-10 day break Read 24 DP Statements

3-Day Review During Break
Day1: Review Exercises 42-36 for 1 hour, 3-7 min per exercise
Day2: Review Exercises 35-29 for 1 hour, 3-7 min per exercise
Day3: Review Exercises 28-22 for 1 hour, 3-7 min per exercise

Visualization Using Numbers
Multiply 7, 14 or 21 numbers every day

	Week 1 and Week 2	Week 3 and Week 4	Week 5 and Week 6
Lesson 3 **Dreams**	Record 1 dream per week	Record 2 dreams per week	Record 3 dreams per week

Week 7
Relive dreams 12 - 1 over 1, 2, or 3 days

	Week 1 and Week 2	Week 3 and Week 4	Week 5 and Week 6
Lesson 4 **Emotions**	Record 1 emotion per day	Record 2 emotions per day	Record 3 emotions per day

Week 7
Relive all emotions over 1, 2, or 3 days

	Week 1 and Week 2	Week 3 and Week 4	Week 5 and Week 6
Lesson 5 **Thoughts**	Record 1 First Answer per day	Record 2 First Answers per day	Record 3 First Answers per day

Week 7
Relive all First Answers over 1, 2, or 3 days

Final Lesson
Continue doing observations, dreams, emotions, thoughts and visualization until you hear your First Self

How To Use The Journal

Read Chapter 38 of Blackroots Science
Read Chapter 39
Read the 'Invocation'
Read Chapter 41
Read Chapter 42

Do Exercise 1, then write down the Observation on page 7 of this Journal.
Fill in the Date, Start Time and End Time of your Observation
Continue similarly with Exercise 2 until Exercise 7

3 days after doing Exercise 7, do recall of Exercise 7 - write it down on page 20 of this Journal.
3 days later do recall of Exercise 6 - write it down on page 18.

Continue similarly until Recall Exercise 1 - write it down on page 8

Then take a 7 - 10 day break then start Exercise 8 etc to the end.

(This Journal was prepared by the webmaster of blackrootscience.com and Sister Tia. We feel this journal is blessed and approved by the First Self to be used by the 144,000 elect because when we finished making it, it ended up with exactly 144 pages, something we did not plan consciously.)

Peace

Invocation

Self of myself, you who knows the hearts and minds of all of us, your descendents, I ask you to guide me in the 2nd level of blackroots science.

My desire is to untangle the knots in my memories. Hidden in them are the precious times you have spoken to me with love, guided me with patience, and blessed me with your sense of peace.

I desire to enter into those precious moments again, so that I can know you consciously and share your indescribable joy.

I will work, even if it's painfully slow, to open the gates of my memories that have been shut tight by the false beliefs imposed on me since I was an innocent child.

    Be with me every step of the way.
    Strengthen my resolve to succeed.
    Increase my patience.
    Open my mind and heart.
    Shower me with your grace.
    Shine your light on every step I take.
    With you always by my side, I will take level 2 to the end and succeed.
    I thank you.

Lesson 1 (Exercises 1 thru 21)

Pick a time interval on the first day of your training between 6pm and midnight. This interval will be about 15 to 30 minutes long.
During this time interval, you'll observe all the details of your own activities, including your surroundings, as they are happening. You'll make a conscious decision to notice as much as possible during the 15-30 min period.
I'll illustrate what I'm asking you to do by way of an example.

Example of Exercise 1
I decided that starting at about 6:15pm until 6:45pm, I'd be noticing everything around me. I did it. Later that night, I wrote the following in my notebook:

Sun Oct 30 2005: I left my house at about 6pm and drove to the park where me and my wife usually walk for exercise. She was busy and couldn't accompany me today. I found a parking space on the street between a red Toyota and a white Ford truck. As I park, it's exactly 6:14pm. I open the trunk and remove my walking shoes and socks and put them on. I put my sandals in the trunk and close it. It's already getting dark. All the squirrels are back up in their trees. I'm greeted by Gordon, a man I usually see here. We exchange a few pleasant words, after which he gets ready to leave. I walk around the park for about 20 minutes, then come back and change my shoes. The truck is gone, but the red car is still here.
It's exactly 6:48pm as I start my car.

As you can see, this is just a normal activity. The difference is that I deliberately decided to become aware of everything going on between 6:14 and 6:48pm, so I could remember it later. It's as simple as that.
So choose a 15-30 min time interval on the first day, between 6pm and midnight. Deliberately notice as much as possible and store it in your memory.
Make sure to notice the EXACT starting and ending time of your observation.
DO NOT WRITE IT DOWN YET.
Write everything you remember just before you go to sleep that same night.
IT'S IMPORTANT TO WRITE IT DOWN JUST BEFORE YOU GO TO BED, WITHIN AN HOUR OR SO, NOT BEFORE THEN.
Here's the most important thing about this simple exercise: It must involve your ACTUAL ACTIVITIES and your memory of them, not your imagination.
DON'T MAKE ANYTHING UP. DON'T INVENT ANY DETAILS.
There's a great difference between real memory and imagination. You must separate them right from the start.
That's it for the first exercise. The second will follow 3 days after the first.
The rest of the first seven Exercises are done the same way. They're all observations 15-30 min long, done between 6pm and midnight, and written down the same night.
In the entire series of lessons we'll use a rhythm of repetition based on the numbers 3,2,1 and 7. This is a natural rhythm that our bodies live by. It's optimally effective for gaining control of our memory circuits in particular and our sensory system in general. In other words, the improvement of memory goes hand in hand with the improvement of perception in general. This is turn will open our so-called 6th sense - our ability to consciously engage in divine communion with the higher Self.
The ultimate goal is to attain our 7th 'sense' - divine unity. That is far in the future for all of us, but there will be unforgettable moments of it along the way.
Exercise 2: Pick a time interval 15-30 min long, between 6pm and midnight, as before. Do this on the 3rd day after Exercise 1. For example, if you did Exercise 1 on a Monday, do #2 on Thursday.
Write down your observation that same night.
Exercise 3: Do 3 days later.
Exercise 4: Do after another 3 days.
Exercise 5,6 and 7: Repeat every 3 days until you've done the 7th exercise.
REMEMBER to notice the EXACT starting and ending times for each one.
REMEMBER to separate FACT from FICTION. If you're in doubt about a particular detail, don't include it.
REMEMBER MOST OF ALL TO BE HONEST TO YOURSELF.

Lesson 1
Stage 1 (Planting Stage)
Do between 6pm and
midnight every 3 days

Date:_____ Start:_____ End:_____

EXERCISE 1

<u>CONSCIOUS OBSERVATION</u>

Recall Exercise 1

Date: _____

Lesson 1
Stage 1 (Planting Stage)
Do between 6pm and
midnight every 3 days

Date:_____ Start:_____ End:_____

EXERCISE 2

CONSCIOUS OBSERVATION

Recall Exercise 2

Date: _____

Lesson 1
Stage 1 (Planting Stage)
Do between 6pm and
midnight every 3 days

Date:_____ Start:_____ End:_____

EXERCISE 3

CONSCIOUS OBSERVATION

Recall Exercise 3

Date: _____

Lesson 1
Stage 1 (Planting Stage)
Do between 6pm and
midnight every 3 days

Date:_____ Start:_____ End:_____

EXERCISE 4

CONSCIOUS OBSERVATION

Recall Exercise 4

Date: _____

Lesson 1
Stage 1 (Planting Stage)
Do between 6pm and midnight every 3 days

Date:_____ Start:_____ End:_____

EXERCISE 5

CONSCIOUS OBSERVATION

Recall Exercise 5

Date: _____

Lesson 1
Stage 1 (Planting Stage)
Do between 6pm and midnight every 3 days

Date:_____ Start:_____ End:_____

EXERCISE 6

CONSCIOUS OBSERVATION

Recall Exercise 6

Date: _____

Lesson 1
Stage 1 (Planting Stage)
Do between 6pm and
midnight every 3 days

Date:_____ Start:_____ End:_____

EXERCISE 7

CONSCIOUS OBSERVATION

Recall Exercise 7

Date: _____

(Take a 7 to 10 day break after the Recalls)

During this break, set aside 7 consecutive nights to read the 12 De-programming Statements. Read all 12 every night for 7 nights straight without missing a night.

12 De-programming Statements

1. I am Black.
2. The original Gods are Black men and women.
3. I am a descendent of the original Gods.
4. My ancestors are the Creators of the universe. They created the earth, the moon, and the stars.
5. They made the non-black races out of their recessive germ.
6. They gave the non-black races power to rule the earth for 6,000 years.
7. The non-black races forced my people into slavery to build their evil and immoral civilization.
8. Their time to rule the earth is now over. Their civilization will fall in my own lifetime.
9. My ancestors built magnificent cities. They built great pyramids and large temples that stood for thousands of years, with granite walls and marble floors, decorated with silver and gold and precious gemstones. I, their descendent, will build more majestic cities for my people.
10. I am one of the 144,000 Black people who will be the new rulers of the earth.
11. We'll make the non-black races our servants. We'll instruct them on how to clean their physical and mental pollution and restore the earth's natural balance.
12. We'll start a new civilization based on good morality. We will rule the earth with a clear mind and a good heart, according to the natural laws of the original Gods.

NOTES

Lesson 1
Stage 2 (Nurturing Stage)
Do between 12noon and
6pm every 2 days

Date:_____ Start:_____ End:_____

EXERCISE 8

CONSCIOUS OBSERVATION

Recall Exercise 8

Date: _____

Lesson 1
Stage 2 (Nurturing Stage)
Do between 12noon and 6pm every 2 days

Date:_____ Start:_____ End:_____

EXERCISE 9

CONSCIOUS OBSERVATION

Recall Exercise 9

Date: _____

Lesson 1
Stage 2 (Nurturing Stage)
Do between 12noon and 6pm every 2 days

Date:_____ Start:_____ End:_____

EXERCISE 10

CONSCIOUS OBSERVATION

Recall Exercise 10

Date: _____

Lesson 1
Stage 2 (Nurturing Stage)
Do between 12noon and 6pm every 2 days

Date: _____ Start: _____ End: _____

EXERCISE 11

<u>CONSCIOUS OBSERVATION</u>

Recall Exercise 11

Date: _____

Lesson 1
Stage 2 (Nurturing Stage)
Do between 12noon and 6pm every 2 days

Date:_____ Start:_____ End:_____

EXERCISE 12

<u>CONSCIOUS OBSERVATION</u>

Recall Exercise 12

Date: _____

Lesson 1
Stage 2 (Nurturing Stage)
Do between 12noon and
6pm every 2 days

Date:_____ Start:_____ End:_____

EXERCISE 13

CONSCIOUS OBSERVATION

Recall Exercise 13

Date:

Lesson 1
Stage 2 (Nurturing Stage)
Do between 12noon and 6pm every 2 days

Date: _____ Start: _____ End: _____

EXERCISE 14

CONSCIOUS OBSERVATION

Recall Exercise 14

Date: _____

(Take a 7 to 10 day break after the Recalls)

During this break, set aside 7 consecutive nights to read the 12 De-programming Statements. Read all 12 every night for 7 nights straight without missing a night.

12 De-programming Statements

1. I am Black.
2. The original Gods are Black men and women.
3. I am a descendent of the original Gods.
4. My ancestors are the Creators of the universe. They created the earth, the moon, and the stars.
5. They made the non-black races out of their recessive germ.
6. They gave the non-black races power to rule the earth for 6,000 years.
7. The non-black races forced my people into slavery to build their evil and immoral civilization.
8. Their time to rule the earth is now over. Their civilization will fall in my own lifetime.
9. My ancestors built magnificent cities. They built great pyramids and large temples that stood for thousands of years, with granite walls and marble floors, decorated with silver and gold and precious gemstones. I, their descendent, will build more majestic cities for my people.
10. I am one of the 144,000 Black people who will be the new rulers of the earth.
11. We'll make the non-black races our servants. We'll instruct them on how to clean their physical and mental pollution and restore the earth's natural balance.
12. We'll start a new civilization based on good morality. We will rule the earth with a clear mind and a good heart, according to the natural laws of the original Gods.

NOTES

Lesson 1
Stage 3 (Harvesting Stage)
Do between 6am and 12noon every day

Date: _____ Start: _____ End: _____

EXERCISE 15

<u>CONSCIOUS OBSERVATION</u>

Recall Exercise 15

Date: _____

Lesson 1
Stage 3 (Harvesting Stage)
Do between 6am and
12noon every day

Date: _____ Start: _____ End: _____

EXERCISE 16

<u>CONSCIOUS OBSERVATION</u>

Recall Exercise 16

Date: _____

Lesson 1
Stage 3 (Harvesting Stage)
Do between 6am and
12noon every day

Date:_____ Start:_____ End:_____

EXERCISE 17

<u>CONSCIOUS OBSERVATION</u>

Blackroots Science Level 2 Journal   43

Recall Exercise 17

Date: _____

Lesson 1
Stage 3 (Harvesting Stage)
Do between 6am and
12noon every day

Date:_____ Start:_____ End:_____

EXERCISE 18

CONSCIOUS OBSERVATION

Recall Exercise 18

Date: _____

Lesson 1
Stage 3 (Harvesting Stage)
Do between 6am and
12noon every day

Date:_____ Start:_____ End:_____

EXERCISE 19

CONSCIOUS OBSERVATION

Recall Exercise 19

Date: _____

Lesson 1
Stage 3 (Harvesting Stage)
Do between 6am and
12noon every day

Date:_____ Start:_____ End:_____

EXERCISE 20

CONSCIOUS OBSERVATION

Recall Exercise 20

Date: _____

Lesson 1
Stage 3 (Harvesting Stage)
Do between 6am and
12noon every day

Date:_____ Start:_____ End:_____

EXERCISE 21

CONSCIOUS OBSERVATION

Recall Exercise 21

Date: _____

(Take a 7 to 10 day break after the Recalls)
Review of Lesson 1

During the 7-10 break, set aside 3 days in which to do a comprehensive review of all the 21 Exercises of Lesson 1.

You'll need 1 hour of quiet, undisturbed time each of the 3 days. (The 3 days don't have to be consecutive; you can spread them out over the 10 day period).

1st day of Re-View

Set aside 1 hour of quiet, undisturbed time to review observations 21 thru 15.

Take 3 to 7 minutes to review each observation. Start with #21, followed by #20, then 19 and so on to #15.

The Re-View will be done in the following way: Find a comfortable place where you can sit undisturbed for up to 1 hour.

Read the first few lines of Exercise 21 to get you started. Then mentally go over observation 21 in as much detail as you can remember. Do not write. Review only in your mind.

In your imagination, see yourself re-living that time period exactly as you experienced it during the actual observation. Let the images of that time gently enter your mind. Spend only 3 to 7 minutes re-living, then rest for 1 minute and go on to the next one.

Read the first few lines of Exercise 20 then re-live it for 3 to 7 minutes the same way, then rest for another minute.

Repeat with observation 19,18,17,16 and 15.

2nd and 3rd day of Re-View

Pick a 2nd day and set aside 1 hr as before, and do #14,13,12,11,10,9 and 8 in that order, resting for a minute in between.

Do the same on the 3rd day, for observations 7 thru 1.

Either sit in front of your computer with all your observations where you can easily read them, or make a printout, and sit in a comfortable place with the printout or notebook in hand.

When you start each Re-View, read the first few lines (Reminder) and try to complete the review. If the memories do not come in a few seconds, don't waste time. Read the entire observation, and then do the Re-living.

You'll notice that the most recent observations are the easiest to remember, and you can probably do all of them just by reading the Reminder. But the older ones are harder. Even so, you'll notice that among the older ones there are some that made a strong impression on your memory.

Review those using only the Reminder. For the rest that are harder to remember, go ahead and read the original observation first, then do the Review.

When you do the reliving, imagine that you are back at that time, reliving the experience. Use your imagination to recall as many details as you can.

Don't spend more than 7 minutes on each one. Rest for 1 minute then go on to the next one.

It's important to go through the process exactly as I've described it.

THE PURPOSE AT THIS EARLY STAGE IS TO OPEN THE GATES OF YOUR MEMORIES SO YOU CAN GO BACK IN TIME CONSCIOUSLY AND IN COMPLETE CONTROL.

During this break, set aside 7 consecutive nights to read the 12 De-programming Statements. Read all 12 every night for 7 nights straight without missing a night.

12 De-programming Statements

1. I am Black.
2. The original Gods are Black men and women.
3. I am a descendent of the original Gods.
4. My ancestors are the Creators of the universe. They created the earth, the moon, and the stars.
5. They made the non-black races out of their recessive germ.
6. They gave the non-black races power to rule the earth for 6,000 years.
7. The non-black races forced my people into slavery to build their evil and immoral civilization.
8. Their time to rule the earth is now over. Their civilization will fall in my own lifetime.
9. My ancestors built magnificent cities. They built great pyramids and large temples that stood for thousands of years, with granite walls and marble floors, decorated with silver and gold and precious gemstones. I, their descendent, will build more majestic cities for my people.
10. I am one of the 144,000 Black people who will be the new rulers of the earth.
11. We'll make the non-black races our servants. We'll instruct them on how to clean their physical and mental pollution and restore the earth's natural balance.
12. We'll start a new civilization based on good morality. We will rule the earth with a clear mind and a good heart, according to the natural laws of the original Gods.

END OF LESSON 1

Read Chapter 47 of Blackroots Science to prepare for Lesson 2

Lesson 2
Stage 1 (Planting Stage)
Do between 12noon and
6pm every 2 days

Date:_____ Start:_____ End:_____

EXERCISE 22
(Notice at least 2 colors)

CONSCIOUS OBSERVATION

Recall Exercise 22

Date: _____

Lesson 2
Stage 1 (Planting Stage)
Do between 12noon and 6pm every 2 days

Date: _____ Start: _____ End: _____

EXERCISE 23

(Notice at least 4 colors)

CONSCIOUS OBSERVATION

Recall Exercise 23

Date: _____

Lesson 2
Stage 1 (Planting Stage)
Do between 12noon and
6pm every 2 days

Date: _____ Start: _____ End: _____

EXERCISE 24

(Notice at least 6 colors)

CONSCIOUS OBSERVATION

Recall Exercise 24

Date: _____

Lesson 2
Stage 1 (Planting Stage)
Do between 12noon and
6pm every 2 days

Date:_____ Start:_____ End:_____

EXERCISE 25
(Notice at least 2 colors and 2 sounds)

CONSCIOUS OBSERVATION

Recall Exercise 25

Date: _____

Lesson 2
Stage 1 (Planting Stage)
Do between 12noon and 6pm every 2 days

Date:_____ Start:_____ End:_____

EXERCISE 26
(Notice at least 4 colors and 4 sounds)

CONSCIOUS OBSERVATION

Recall Exercise 26

Date: _____

Lesson 2
Stage 1 (Planting Stage)
Do between 12noon and
6pm every 2 days

Date: _____ Start: _____ End: _____

EXERCISE 27
(Notice at least 6 colors and 6 sounds)

CONSCIOUS OBSERVATION

Recall Exercise 27

Date: _____

Lesson 2
Stage 1 (Planting Stage)
Do between 12noon and
6pm every 2 days

Date:_____ Start:_____ End:_____

EXERCISE 28
(Notice at least 8 colors and 8 sounds)

CONSCIOUS OBSERVATION

Recall Exercise 28

Date: _____

(Take a 7 to 10 day break after the Recalls)

During the break, read the 24 De-Programming Statements below. Set aside 7 consecutive nights to read them, and read them for 7 straight nights without missing a night.

24 De-programming Statements

1. I am Black.
2. The original Gods are Black men and women.
3. I am a descendent of the original Gods.
4. My ancestors are the Creators of the universe. They created the earth, the moon, and the stars.
5. They made the non-black races out of their recessive germ.
6. They gave the non-black races power to rule the earth for 6,000 years.
7. The non-black races forced my people into slavery to build their evil and immoral civilization.
8. Their time to rule the earth is now over. Their civilization will fall in my own lifetime.
9. My ancestors built magnificent cities. They built great pyramids and large temples that stood for thousands of years, with granite walls and marble floors, decorated with silver and gold and precious gemstones. I, their descendent, will build more majestic cities for my people.
10. I am one of the 144,000 Black people who will be the new rulers of the earth.
11. We'll make the non-black races our servants. We'll instruct them on how to clean their physical and mental pollution and restore the earth's natural balance.
12. We'll start a new civilization based on good morality. We will rule the earth with a clear mind and a good heart, according to the natural laws of the original Gods.
13. Black people are causal beings: non-blacks are symptomatic beings. Black people can see the true causes of things, whereas non-blacks see only the symptoms.
14. Black people cure illnesses and problems by preventing the cause; non-blacks alleviate illnesses and problems by treating the symptoms.
15. The god of the non-black races is greed. If they're not stopped, they will go to any extreme to satisfy this god, even to the extreme of destroying the earth and all life on it.
16. Because they worship greed, their economic system is based on its satisfaction.
17. Their political legal and religious systems are used to protect their economic system so they can better pursue their god who is insatiable.
18. They have no regard for human life and other life if it stands in the way of satisfying their greed, which is like a bottomless pit.
19. When the damage caused by their economic system becomes obvious to all, they cover it up by treating the symptoms, while continuing the actions that caused the damage.
20. Their medical system is a clear example of their symptomatic nature. They put poisons like processed sugar in foods, chemicals in soil and water, and smog in the air, not to mention noise pollution and mental pollution due to their perversions. When the inevitable illnesses come, they 'cure' them by prescribing other poisons to treat the symptoms, while they continue to pour more poisons into the systems.
21. This behavior is driven by their greed. It's the quickest way to make money. They use this money to try and fill the bottomless pit in them, which is slowly but surely consuming them.
22. Money is energy. Money that is used for the satisfaction of greed is energy wasted in a vicious and destructive cycle. This cycle threatens to destroy not only the worshippers of greed, but Black people also.
23. Only the causal beings - Black people - can prevent this impending disaster. We will uproot the cause of the problem, not just treat the symptoms. The cause of all the world's problems is the rulership of the non-blacks.
24. We in this group are part of the 144,000 Black people who will rule the earth. All the world's problems and illnesses will end when we take over rulership, and remove the non-blacks from the face of the earth and the face of the universe.

NOTES

Lesson 2
 Stage 2 (Nurturing Stage)
 Do between 6pm and
 midnight every 3 days

Date:_____ Start:_____ End:_____

EXERCISE 29
(Notice at least 6 colors, 6 sounds and 2 smells)

CONSCIOUS OBSERVATION

Recall Exercise 29

Date: _____

Lesson 2
Stage 2 (Nurturing Stage)
Do between 6pm and midnight every 3 days

Date:_____ Start:_____ End:_____

EXERCISE 30
(Notice at least 6 colors, 6 sounds and 4 smells)

CONSCIOUS OBSERVATION

Recall Exercise 30

Date: _____

Lesson 2
Stage 2 (Nurturing Stage)
Do between 6pm and
midnight every 3 days

Date: _____ Start: _____ End: _____

EXERCISE 31
(Notice at least 6 colors, 6 sounds and 6 smells)

CONSCIOUS OBSERVATION

Recall Exercise 31

Date: _____

Lesson 2
 Stage 2 (Nurturing Stage)
Do between 6pm and
midnight every 3 days

Date:_____ Start:_____ End:_____

EXERCISE 32
(Notice at least 6 colors, 6 sounds, 6 smells and 2 touches)

CONSCIOUS OBSERVATION

Recall Exercise 32

Date: _____

Lesson 2
Stage 2 (Nurturing Stage)
Do between 6pm and
midnight every 3 days

Date:_____ Start:_____ End:_____

EXERCISE 33
(Notice at least 6 colors, 6 sounds, 6 smells and 4 touches)

<u>CONSCIOUS OBSERVATION</u>

Recall Exercise 33

Date: _____

Lesson 2
Stage 2 (Nurturing Stage)
Do between 6pm and
midnight every 3 days

Date:_____ Start:_____ End:_____

EXERCISE 34
(Notice at least 6 colors, 6 sounds, 6 smells and 6 touches)

<u>CONSCIOUS OBSERVATION</u>

Recall Exercise 34

Date: _____

Lesson 2
 Stage 2 (Nurturing Stage)
 Do between 6pm and
 midnight every 3 days

Date:_____ Start:_____ End:_____

EXERCISE 35
(Notice at least 8 colors, 8 sounds, 8 smells and 8 touches)

CONSCIOUS OBSERVATION

Recall Exercise 35

Date: _____

(Take a 7 to 10 day break after the Recalls)

During the break, read the 24 De-Programming Statements below. Set aside 7 consecutive nights to read them, and read them for 7 straight nights without missing a night.

24 De-programming Statements

1. I am Black.
2. The original Gods are Black men and women.
3. I am a descendent of the original Gods.
4. My ancestors are the Creators of the universe. They created the earth, the moon, and the stars.
5. They made the non-black races out of their recessive germ.
6. They gave the non-black races power to rule the earth for 6,000 years.
7. The non-black races forced my people into slavery to build their evil and immoral civilization.
8. Their time to rule the earth is now over. Their civilization will fall in my own lifetime.
9. My ancestors built magnificent cities. They built great pyramids and large temples that stood for thousands of years, with granite walls and marble floors, decorated with silver and gold and precious gemstones. I, their descendent, will build more majestic cities for my people.
10. I am one of the 144,000 Black people who will be the new rulers of the earth.
11. We'll make the non-black races our servants. We'll instruct them on how to clean their physical and mental pollution and restore the earth's natural balance.
12. We'll start a new civilization based on good morality. We will rule the earth with a clear mind and a good heart, according to the natural laws of the original Gods.
13. Black people are causal beings: non-blacks are symptomatic beings. Black people can see the true causes of things, whereas non-blacks see only the symptoms.
14. Black people cure illnesses and problems by preventing the cause; non-blacks alleviate illnesses and problems by treating the symptoms.
15. The god of the non-black races is greed. If they're not stopped, they will go to any extreme to satisfy this god, even to the extreme of destroying the earth and all life on it.
16. Because they worship greed, their economic system is based on its satisfaction.
17. Their political legal and religious systems are used to protect their economic system so they can better pursue their god who is insatiable.
18. They have no regard for human life and other life if it stands in the way of satisfying their greed, which is like a bottomless pit.
19. When the damage caused by their economic system becomes obvious to all, they cover it up by treating the symptoms, while continuing the actions that caused the damage.
20. Their medical system is a clear example of their symptomatic nature. They put poisons like processed sugar in foods, chemicals in soil and water, and smog in the air, not to mention noise pollution and mental pollution due to their perversions. When the inevitable illnesses come, they 'cure' them by prescribing other poisons to treat the symptoms, while they continue to pour more poisons into the systems.
21. This behavior is driven by their greed. It's the quickest way to make money. They use this money to try and fill the bottomless pit in them, which is slowly but surely consuming them.
22. Money is energy. Money that is used for the satisfaction of greed is energy wasted in a vicious and destructive cycle. This cycle threatens to destroy not only the worshippers of greed, but Black people also.
23. Only the causal beings - Black people - can prevent this impending disaster. We will uproot the cause of the problem, not just treat the symptoms. The cause of all the world's problems is the rulership of the non-blacks.
24. We in this group are part of the 144,000 Black people who will rule the earth. All the world's problems and illnesses will end when we take over rulership, and remove the non-blacks from the face of the earth and the face of the universe.

(Start to do Visualization Using Numbers every day)

Every morning after you get up, take 5 minutes to multiply these numbers in your head. You may start this at any time during the break.
You have the choice to either do 7, 14, or 21 multiplications each morning. (Each line of numbers has 7 multiplications; two lines have 14 and 3 lines have 21. So do either 1 or 2 or 3 lines each day). If you start with 7 multiplications, you can increase it later on. The minimum is to start with 7.
If you're comfortable with numbers, do 14 every morning. If your mind is naturally gifted with numbers, do 21 multiplications (3 lines) in the group each morning.
From group 1, copy the first line (or 2, or 3) onto a piece of paper. As soon as you get the chance after waking up, before eating anything, take a few minutes to do the multiplications in your head.
The 1st group is fairly easy to multiply. They're just for getting you started.
Do them on the 1st morning. Do the same with the 2nd group.
The visualization begins with the 3rd group (beginning with 23x4).
Starting with the 3rd group, you MUST LOOK AWAY (OR CLOSE YOUR EYES) when multiplying. Look at the first number (23x4) then look away (or close your eyes) and multiply it in your head. Do the same for all the numbers to follow.
Don't spend more than 5 minutes each morning, regardless of whether you do 7, 14, or 21 multiplications.
After 5 minutes, let it go no matter how few you've done.

Method of Multiplication/Visualization
When you get to the 3rd group (beginning with 23x4), use the following method to multiply: Look once at the number 23x4.
Then LOOK AWAY OR CLOSE YOUR EYES, and do the following in your head: Take 23 and change it to 20 and 3. Multiply 20x4 (=80) and 3x4 (=12) then add the two answers (80+12 = 92).
This method is useful for both visualization and memory. Separating 23 into 20 and 3 trains the imagination to visualize, remember and process two or more things at the same time. The 3-step process will help you to somehow train yourself to visualize. To help you in the beginning, you can remind yourself by saying the numbers silently or out loud. But later try and remember them without saying them to yourself.
Write the answers next to each one and then check them with your calculator .
Don't rush it. Do it slowly and deliberately, always keeping the images in your mind at every step. The purpose is not to turn you into a math wiz, but to be able to visualize and remember. This is crucial for all forms of memory recall.
Some of you will find this easy to do while others will struggle at first. If you struggle, then do only 7 every morning, and stay with the same group until you feel comfortable with them.
Again, don't spend more than 5 minutes each morning.
As soon as you finish all seven groups and you're satisfied that you can comfortably multiply them in your head, then check the website for more numbers, or make up your own.
Here are the 7 groups of numbers. Each group has 21 multiplications. Do either 7, 14, or all 21 every day.
(The sets of numbers can be found on the website: blackrootscience.com/visualization.html)

Lesson 2
Stage 3 (Harvesting Stage)
Do between 12 noon and 6pm every 2 days

Date:_____ Start:_____ End:_____

EXERCISE 36
(Notice at least 8 colors, 8 sounds, 6 touches and 2 smells)

CONSCIOUS OBSERVATION

Recall Exercise 36

Date:

Lesson 2
Stage 3 (Harvesting Stage)
Do between 12 noon and
6pm every 2 days

Date:_____ Start:_____ End:_____

EXERCISE 37
(Notice at least 8 colors, 8 sounds, 6 touches, 2 smells and 2 tastes)

CONSCIOUS OBSERVATION

Recall Exercise 37

Date: _____

Lesson 2
Stage 3 (Harvesting Stage)
Do between 12 noon and 6pm every 2 days

Date:_____ Start:_____ End:_____

EXERCISE 38
(Notice at least 8 colors, 8 sounds, 6 touches, 4 smells and 2 tastes)

CONSCIOUS OBSERVATION

Recall Exercise 38

Date: _____

Lesson 2
Stage 3 (Harvesting Stage)
Do between 12 noon and 6pm every 2 days

Date:_____ Start:_____ End:_____

EXERCISE 39
(Notice at least 8 colors, 8 sounds, 8 touches, 4 smells and 2 tastes)

<u>CONSCIOUS OBSERVATION</u>

Recall Exercise 39

Date: _____

Lesson 2
Stage 3 (Harvesting Stage)
Do between 12 noon and
6pm every 2 days

Date: _____ Start: _____ End: _____

EXERCISE 40
(Notice at least 8 colors, 8 sounds, 8 touches, 4 smells and 2 tastes)

CONSCIOUS OBSERVATION

Recall Exercise 40

Date: _____

Lesson 2
Stage 3 (Harvesting Stage)
Do between 12 noon and
6pm every 2 days

Date:_____ Start:_____ End:_____

EXERCISE 41
(Notice at least 8 colors, 8 sounds, 8 touches, 6 smells and 2 tastes)

<u>CONSCIOUS OBSERVATION</u>

Recall Exercise 41

Date: _____

Lesson 2
Stage 3 (Harvesting Stage)
Do between 12 noon and 6pm every 2 days

Date:_____ Start:_____ End:_____

EXERCISE 42
(Notice at least 8 colors, 8 sounds, 8 touches, 6 smells and 4 tastes)

CONSCIOUS OBSERVATION

Recall Exercise 42

Date: _____

Review of Lesson 2

Take a 7-10 day break period before Lesson 3, during which you do all the Recalls of Lesson 2. Use 1 hour per day for 3 days, going through lessons 42-36 on the 1st day, then 35-29 on the 2nd day, then 28-22 on the last day, as you did at the end of Lesson 1.

During the break, read the 24 De-Programming Statements below. Set aside 7 consecutive nights to read them, and read them for 7 straight nights without missing a night.

24 De-programming Statements

1. I am Black.
2. The original Gods are Black men and women.
3. I am a descendent of the original Gods.
4. My ancestors are the Creators of the universe. They created the earth, the moon, and the stars.
5. They made the non-black races out of their recessive germ.
6. They gave the non-black races power to rule the earth for 6,000 years.
7. The non-black races forced my people into slavery to build their evil and immoral civilization.
8. Their time to rule the earth is now over. Their civilization will fall in my own lifetime.
9. My ancestors built magnificent cities. They built great pyramids and large temples that stood for thousands of years, with granite walls and marble floors, decorated with silver and gold and precious gemstones. I, their descendent, will build more majestic cities for my people.
10. I am one of the 144,000 Black people who will be the new rulers of the earth.
11. We'll make the non-black races our servants. We'll instruct them on how to clean their physical and mental pollution and restore the earth's natural balance.
12. We'll start a new civilization based on good morality. We will rule the earth with a clear mind and a good heart, according to the natural laws of the original Gods.
13. Black people are causal beings: non-blacks are symptomatic beings. Black people can see the true causes of things, whereas non-blacks see only the symptoms.
14. Black people cure illnesses and problems by preventing the cause; non-blacks alleviate illnesses and problems by treating the symptoms.
15. The god of the non-black races is greed. If they're not stopped, they will go to any extreme to satisfy this god, even to the extreme of destroying the earth and all life on it.
16. Because they worship greed, their economic system is based on its satisfaction.
17. Their political legal and religious systems are used to protect their economic system so they can better pursue their god who is insatiable.
18. They have no regard for human life and other life if it stands in the way of satisfying their greed, which is like a bottomless pit.
19. When the damage caused by their economic system becomes obvious to all, they cover it up by treating the symptoms, while continuing the actions that caused the damage.
20. Their medical system is a clear example of their symptomatic nature. They put poisons like processed sugar in foods, chemicals in soil and water, and smog in the air, not to mention noise pollution and mental pollution due to their perversions. When the inevitable illnesses come, they 'cure' them by prescribing other poisons to treat the symptoms, while they continue to pour more poisons into the systems.
21. This behavior is driven by their greed. It's the quickest way to make money. They use this money to try and fill the bottomless pit in them, which is slowly but surely consuming them.
22. Money is energy. Money that is used for the satisfaction of greed is energy wasted in a vicious and destructive cycle. This cycle threatens to destroy not only the worshippers of greed, but Black people also.
23. Only the causal beings - Black people - can prevent this impending disaster. We will uproot the cause of the problem, not just treat the symptoms. The cause of all the world's problems is the rulership of the non-blacks.
24. We in this group are part of the 144,000 Black people who will rule the earth. All the world's problems and illnesses will end when we take over rulership, and remove the non-blacks from the face of the earth and the face of the universe.

END OF LESSON 2

LESSON 3

DREAM EXERCISES

Start after the break.
Once a week, for 2 weeks, record your dreams of the night before as soon as you wake up. If you wake up in the middle of the night after a particularly clear dream, make some quick notes of the major points, and then write it in full detail when you get the chance the next morning. It's important to record the details as soon as you can because as you know, dream memories can fade rather quickly.
After 2 weeks, record your dreams twice a week for 2 weeks.
After another 2 weeks, record them 3 times a week for 2 weeks.

To make it more plain:
Week 1: Record your dreams of any 1 night of that week
Week 2: Same as week 1
Week 3: Record the dreams any 2 nights of that week
Week 4: Same as week 3
Week 5: Any 3 nights
Week 6: Same as week 5
Week 7: Go over your dreams of the last 6 weeks, reliving them in as much detail as possible. You can do the recalls all in 1 day, or spread them over 2 or 3 days, no more than 3 days. Use the first few lines to remind yourself, or read all of it if you don't remember.
There should be at least 12 dreams. If you have a hard time remembering your dreams, record the feelings you have after you think you had a dream.
Dreams will always leave you with strong emotions, either joy, sadness, fear, dread, worry, etc. Describe what you feel as clearly as you can, then relive the emotions and dreams you remember in the 7th week.
At this point don't try too hard to interpret your dreams, unless the meaning is crystal clear. The meaning of your dreams will become clear the longer you record and recall them.
Take about a 7-10 day break before lesson 4. During that break, read the 24 De-Programming Statements once every night for 7 nights. Try not to miss a night.

Lesson 3
Dream Exercises
Record 1 dream this week

Week 1.

Date: _____

DREAM

Lesson 3 | Week 2. | Date:_____
Dream Exercises
Record 1 dream this week

DREAM

Lesson 3
Dream Exercises
Record 2 dreams this week

Week 3.

Date:_____

DREAM 1

Lesson 3
Dream Exercises
Record 2 dreams this week

Week 3.

Date:_____

DREAM 2

Lesson 3
Dream Exercises
Record 2 dreams this week

Week 4.

Date: _____

DREAM 1

Lesson 3
Dream Exercises
Record 2 dreams this week

Week 4.

Date:_____

DREAM 2

Lesson 3
Dream Exercises
Record 3 dreams this week

Week 5.

Date:_____

DREAM 1

Lesson 3
Dream Exercises
Record 3 dreams this week

Week 5.

Date:_____

DREAM 2

Lesson 3
Dream Exercises
Record 3 dreams this week

Week 5.

Date:_____

DREAM 3

Lesson 3
Dream Exercises
Record 3 dreams this week

Week 6.

Date:_____

DREAM 1

Lesson 3
Dream Exercises
Record 3 dreams this week

Week 6.

Date:_____

DREAM 2

Lesson 3
Dream Exercises
Record 3 dreams this week

Week 6.

Date:_____

DREAM 3

WEEK 7 - RECALLS

(Read the 24 De-Programming Statements for 7 days)

Recall all 12 dreams over 1, 2, or 3 days

Brother Blackroots did not specify if we should write down the dream recalls, nevertheless he did say in Chapter 47 paragraph 3, *'Beginning in Lesson 2 we're going to reduce writing to a minimum, so we can rely more on our minds'*. If you want to write your dream recalls, do so in a separate notebook.

END OF LESSON 3

LESSON 4

EMOTIONS

(Continue to record your dreams about 3 times every week.)

Lesson 4: Feelings

Week 1: At night, write down 1 strong feeling that you had that day, whether it's joy, anger, sadness, peace, etc. Do this for 7 days. Briefly describe the circumstances that led to the feeling.
Week 2: Same as week 1
Week 3: Record 2 clear emotions every day for 7 days, along with a brief description of the circumstances surrounding them.
Week 4: Same as in week 3
Week 5: Record 3 emotions of each day, for 7 days
Week 6: Same as in week 5
Week 7: Go over your recalls same as in lesson 3
Take a 7-10 day break and read the DP Statements for 7 nights.

Lesson 4
Emotions
Record 1 emotion per day this week

Week 1.   Start Date: _____   End Date: _____

1

2

3

4

5

6

7

Blackroots Science Level 2 Journal   117

Lesson 4
Emotions
Record 1 emotion per day this week

Week 2. Start Date: _____ End Date: _____

1 _____

2 _____

3 _____

4 _____

5 _____

6 _____

7 _____

Lesson 4
Emotions
Record 2 emotions per day this week

Week 3.   Start Date: _____   End Date: _____

1

2

3

4

5

6

7

8.

9.

10.

11.

12.

13.

14.

Lesson 4
Emotions
Record 2 emotions per day this week

Week 4.   Start Date: _____   End Date: _____

1

2

3

4

5

6

7

8

9

10

11

12

13

14

Lesson 4
Emotions
Record 3 emotions per day this week

Week 5.   Start Date: _____   End Date: _____

1

2

3

4

5

6

7

8

9

10

11

12

13

14

15.

16.

17.

18.

19.

20.

21.

Lesson 4
Emotions
Record 3 emotions per day this week

Week 6.   Start Date: _____   End Date: _____

1

2

3

4

5

6

7

8

9

10

11

12

13

14

15

16

17

18

19

20

21

WEEK 7 - RECALLS

(Read the 24 De-Programming Statements for 7 days)

Recall all emotions over 1, 2, or 3 days

Brother Blackroots did not specify if we should write down the emotion recalls, nevertheless he did say in Chapter 47 paragraph 3, *'Beginning in Lesson 2 we're going to reduce writing to a minimum, so we can rely more on our minds'*. If you want to write your emotion recalls, do so in a separate notebook.

END OF LESSON 4

LESSON 5

THOUGHTS

(Continue to record you dreams and emotions at least 3 times a week, as many dreams as you can remember from each of the 3 nights, and as many feelings as you can remember from each of the 3 days of each week. Try to do dreams and feelings on the same day, i.e record the feelings before going to bed, then the dreams the following morning)

Lesson 5: Thoughts

Week 1: Listen carefully to the FIRST ANSWER that comes to your mind whenever you ask yourself a question. Even if you decide not to act according to the ANSWER, pay attention to it and remember it. Memorize it and record it at night, with a brief description of the question you were wondering about, and what you decided to do.

EXAMPLE: What should I wear today?
FIRST ANSWER: Wear your blue pants/blue dress etc. (I decided to wear the grey pants/yellow dress instead.)
Do this every day for 7 days
Week 2: Same as in week 1
Week 3: Record 2 FIRST ANSWERS each day for 7 days, along with the circumstances and your final decision
Week 4: Same as in week 3
Week 5: Record 3 FIRST ANSWERS each day for 7 days, along with the circumstances and your final decision
Week 6: Same as week 5
Week 7: Do a recall of the thoughts of the last 6 weeks, consulting your notes.
Take a 7 to 10 day break during which you read the 24 DP Statements.

Final Lesson: Continue as long as is necessary with the recording of your dreams, feelings, and thoughts at least 3 times a week.

Lesson 5
Thoughts
Record 1 First Answer per day this week

Week 1.   Start Date: _____ End Date: _____

1

2

3

4

5

6

7

Lesson 5
Thoughts
Record 1 First Answer per day this week

Week 2.   Start Date:_____   End Date:_____

1 _____

2 _____

3 _____

4 _____

5 _____

6 _____

7 _____

Lesson 5
Thoughts
Record 2 First Answers per day this week

Week 3.   Start Date: _____   End Date: _____

1

2

3

4

5

6

7

8

9

10

11

12

13

14

Lesson 5
Thoughts
Record 2 First Answers per day this week

Week 4.   Start Date: _____ End Date: _____

1 _____

2 _____

3 _____

4 _____

5 _____

6 _____

7 _____

8.

9.

10.

11.

12.

13.

14.

Lesson 5
Thoughts
Record 3 First Answers per day this week

Week 5.   Start Date: _____   End Date: _____

1

2

3

4

5

6

7

Blackroots Science Level 2 Journal

8

9

10

11

12

13

14

15.

16.

17.

18.

19.

20.

21.

Lesson 5
Thoughts
Record 3 First Answers per day this week

Week 6.   Start Date: _____ End Date: _____

1

2

3

4

5

6

7

8

9

10

11

12

13

14

15.

16.

17.

18.

19.

20.

21.

WEEK 7 - RECALLS

(Read the 24 De-Programming Statements for 7 days)

Recall all First Answers over 1, 2, or 3 days

Brother Blackroots did not specify if we should write down the thought recalls, nevertheless he did say in Chapter 47 paragraph 3, *'Beginning in Lesson 2 we're going to reduce writing to a minimum, so we can rely more on our minds'*. If you want to write your thought recalls, do so in a separate notebook.

END OF LESSON 5

KEEP DOING LEVEL 2 UNTIL YOU HEAR THE FIRST SELF

PEACE

NOTES

Made in the USA
Monee, IL
25 November 2024

71195510R00090